the big risk

a book about trust

by William Peil

ABBEY PRESS

St. Meinrad, Indiana 47577

Library of Congress Catalog Number
88-72372

ISBN 0-87029-218-8

Foreword

The struggle to trust is universal—and life-long.

We seem to be born with trust, but then something happens and many of us lose it. We never want to trust anyone again—God, or people, or self.

To be without trust is to live in torment.

This booklet is an attempt to help people who find it hard to trust.

I have trusted myself to succeed.

My thanks to all who helped, especially children and other friends.

William Peil

Mary
was a teen-aged girl
from a small town.

NAZARETH

TOWN
WELL

A messenger
from God told her . . .

. . . and it worked out *fine!*

Joseph
understood

people
accepted

and Jesus got his chance
to share his life and his talents
with the world.

Mary of Nazareth
trusted not only God.
She also trusted *herself.*

Mary trusted *not only*
God and self; she also
trusted others.
She trusted Joseph.

His mother raised
Jesus well and taught
him about **TRUST.**

Nobody trusted God,
self, and others better
than Jesus.

#1

TRUSTER

JESUS   OF   NAZARETH

Still, it was a
life-long struggle
for him—trusting God

trusting self

trusting others

But he did it,
and spent himself
doing it to the end.

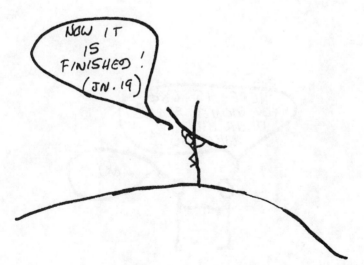

Trusting

is putting something in
somebody's hands
knowing that person
will take care of it.

Trusting

God

is putting

my disappointments
my trials
my sicknesses
my setbacks
my losses
my mistakes
my failures
even my sins,

in his hands,
knowing he'll take care of them.

For those
who trust God . . .

All
things

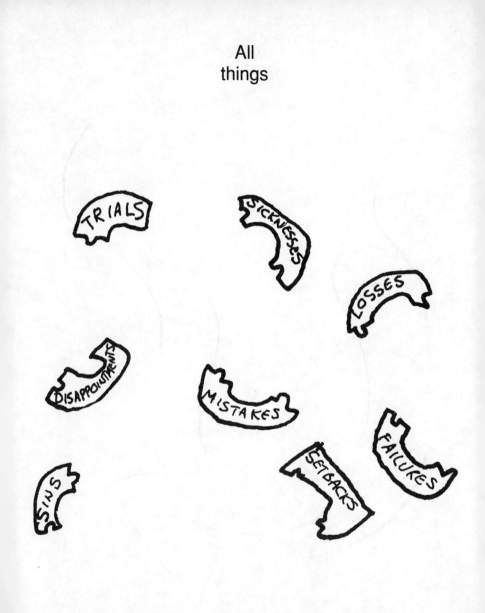

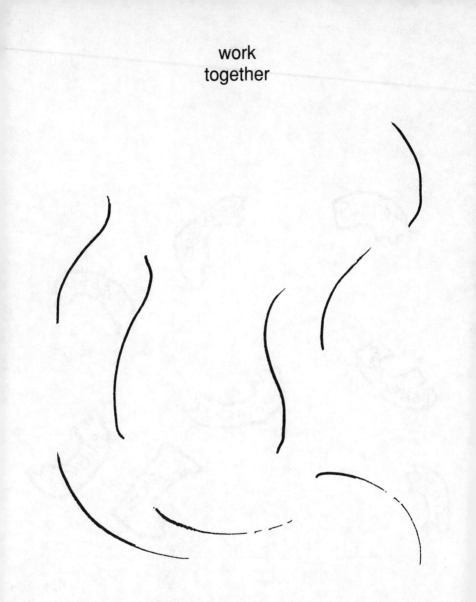

unto

Not always
the way WE want,
but for GOOD.

Some quotes to think about
on trusting God,
from David of Bethlehem:

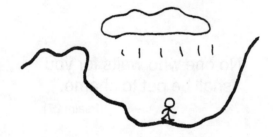

"Even though I walk
in the dark valley
I fear no evil.
You are at my side."

(Psalm 23)

"O Lord,
in you I trust,

No one who waits for you
shall be put to shame."

(Psalm 27)

"Your judgment
is on those
who worship
vain idols,

but my trust
is in
the Lord."
(Psalm 31)

"Neither in
my youth

nor now
that I am old

have I seen
a just person
forsaken."
(Psalm 37)

"Some are
strong in chariots,
some in horses.

But we
are strong in
the name
of the Lord."

(Psalm 22)

"Like a
weaned child in
its mother's lap,

so is my soul
within me."

(Psalm 131)

Trusting

self

is putting something
in my own hands,
knowing I'll take care of it:

my job
my assets
my choices
my feelings
my needs.

Maybe I'll quit
the job.

Maybe I'll decide
to express my
anger appropriately.

Maybe I'll tell someone what I need and not just make them guess at it.

Maybe I'll agree with someone's view of my assets

Whatever it is
that happens,
I'll take care of it!

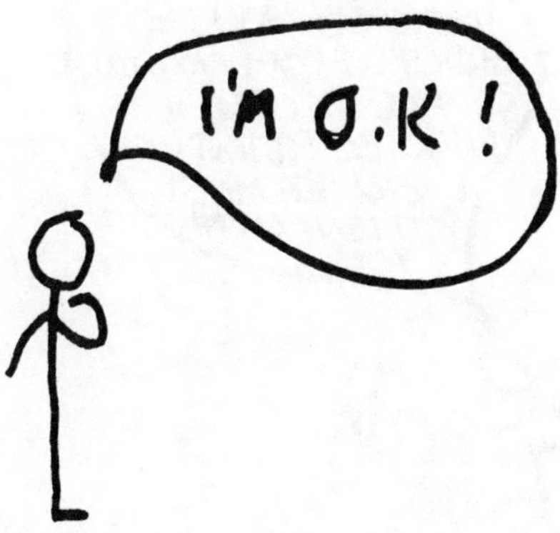

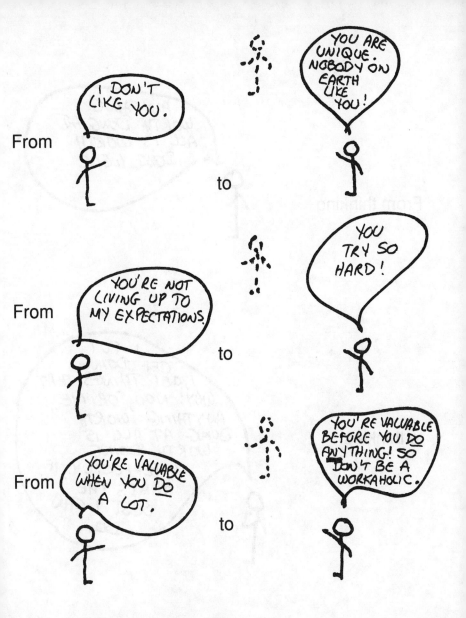

From thinking

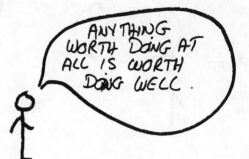

to thinking

From thinking

to thinking

From thinking

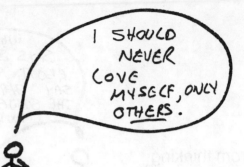

to thinking

From thinking

to thinking

Trusting

others

is putting something
in someone else's hands,
knowing that person
will take care of it:

my heart
my fears
my needs
my secrets
my thoughts

It is true,
some people I need
to check out first.

I may *feel* safe
if I don't
trust anybody,
but it's the safety
of a coffin

with the lid pulled
down on top of me
in the darkness.

Some people
may let me down
and I'll never want
to trust again, but there's
more life in a

broken heart
than in a

frozen heart.

Some ways
to move towards
trusting others:

From thinking

to thinking

From thinking

to thinking

From thinking

to thinking

From thinking

to thinking

From thinking

to thinking

It's
a

risk

to

trust

God
or self
or people

But if
I don't risk,

if I'm not willing to lose,
I'll never win.
"He who only seeks
to save his life will lose it."
(Mark 8:35)

But if I do risk,
I may find some
good things.

A person without
any one of
the three trusts
is dying inside,

and is in misery.

The never-ending
struggle to trust
is *important.*

Psalm 116
A summary of the life
of Jesus, probably sung by him
and his 12 friends at
his last meal on earth.

(Mk. 14:26)

"I trusted,
even when I said:
'I am GREATLY
AFFLICTED!'
and, in my alarm,
'NO ONE IS
DEPENDABLE!'

How shall I make
a return to the Lord
for all the good he
had done for me?

The CUP OF
SALVATION I will
take up and call
on the name
of the Lord!

48

My VOWS to the Lord
I will pay in the
PRESENCE OF
all HIS PEOPLE.

PRECIOUS in the
eyes of the Lord
is the DEATH of his
FAITHFUL ones.

O Lord, I am
your SERVANT,
SON OF YOUR
HANDMAID. You
have LOOSED
MY BONDS.

49

To you will I offer
A SACRIFICE
of thanksgiving and
I will CALL ON the
NAME OF THE LORD.

My VOWS to the
Lord I will pay
in the
PRESENCE
of all
HIS PEOPLE,
in the
courts of the Lord,
in your midst,
O JERUSALEM."

50

Prayer for Trust

Lord, from whom we have
all come, help me to
trust you, myself, and
others. Give me the
courage to risk that
Jesus of Nazareth had,
and his will to struggle
to the end. I put
everything in your hands.
Take care of it.
Amen.